CODING: A BEGINNER'S GUIDE TO MASTERING THE ART

ANIK CHAKRABORTY

Made with ♥ on the Notion Press Platform
www.notionpress.com

I am writing this book with the intention of sharing my knowledge and experience with others who are just starting on their coding journey. This book is dedicated to all the juniors and coding enthusiasts who are eager to learn and master the art of coding. My hope is that by reading this book, you will gain a comprehensive understanding of coding, from the basics to advanced topics, and be inspired to continue learning and growing as a developer. Whether you are a beginner or an experienced programmer looking to brush up on your skills, I believe this book will provide valuable insights and guidance to help you reach your goals.

Contents

Contents

Foreword

In today's rapidly evolving technology landscape, coding has become an essential skill for individuals and businesses alike. As technology continues to play an increasingly important role in our daily lives, understanding how to code has become a critical component in personal and professional growth. With "Coding: A Beginner's Guide to Mastering the Art," author Anik Chakraborty offers a comprehensive and accessible guide to coding, designed for those new to the field as well as experienced coders seeking to expand their skillset.

Anik's extensive experience in the industry and passion for coding shines through in every chapter of this book. With a focus on clarity and simplicity, he breaks down complex concepts into easy-to-understand language, making coding accessible to anyone with a desire to learn. Whether you're a student looking to pursue a career in tech or a professional looking to upskill, "Coding: A Beginner's Guide to Mastering the Art" provides an invaluable resource for anyone seeking to develop their coding skills.

I highly recommend this book to anyone looking to embark on the exciting journey of learning to code. With Anik's expert guidance and practical insights, you'll gain a solid foundation in the essential concepts of coding and be well on your way to becoming a confident and skilled coder.

Preface

It is with great pleasure that I introduce this book, "Coding: A Beginner's Guide to Mastering the Art." My name is Anik Chakraborty with a YouTube channel Named (TechWithAnik), I am a seasoned software developer with over 5 years of experience in the field of coding. Throughout my career, I have honed my skills in multiple programming languages and have completed more than 25 successful projects. My expertise and attention to detail have allowed me to work with a diverse range of clients and provide them with high-quality solutions to meet their needs.

I am passionate about coding and am always striving to expand my knowledge and stay current with the latest technologies and best practices in the industry. This passion for coding has driven me to write this book, which is aimed at those who are new to the world of coding. My goal is to provide a comprehensive and easy-to-follow guide that will help you develop the skills and knowledge you need to become a confident and successful coder.

Whether you are a complete beginner or have some basic knowledge of coding, this book will provide you with the tools and guidance you need to take your coding skills to the next level. Each chapter is designed to build upon the previous one, taking you from the basics of coding to more advanced topics with a proper roadmap.

So, if you are ready to embark on the exciting journey of coding, let's get started!

Acknowledgements

As I sit down to write this book, I am filled with gratitude for all of the people who have supported and encouraged me along the way. This book would not have been possible without their contributions and their belief in my abilities.

I would like to express my deepest thanks to my family for their unwavering support and for always being my biggest cheerleaders. Their love and encouragement have been a source of strength and inspiration throughout this journey.

I would also like to extend my gratitude to my teachers, mentors & YouTubers in the coding industry. Their knowledge, experience, and insights have been invaluable in shaping my understanding of the subject and have helped me grow as a developer.

Finally, I would like to thank the coding community for being such a supportive and inclusive group of individuals. I have learned so much from others in the community and am grateful for the opportunities to collaborate and share ideas with others who share my passion for coding.

I am truly grateful to everyone who has played a role in the creation of this book and am proud to share it with the world. Thank you all for your support and encouragement.

Prologue

The world of coding is a vast and ever-evolving landscape. As technology continues to advance, the demand for skilled software developers continues to grow, making coding a valuable and in-demand skill. Whether you're a complete beginner or have some experience, this book offers a comprehensive guide to mastering the art of coding. From setting up your environment to developing a complete project, you'll learn the key concepts, best practices, and advanced topics in the world of coding.

The author, Anik Chakraborty, is a seasoned software developer with over 5 years of experience in the field. With a wealth of knowledge and a passion for coding, Anik has written this book as a guide for anyone interested in learning the fundamentals of coding, from the basics to the most advanced concepts.

Whether you're looking to start a new career in tech, or simply interested in learning a new skill, this book is the perfect resource to get you started on your coding journey. So buckle up, grab your favorite beverage, and let's get started!

CHAPTER ONE

INTRODUCTION: WHAT IS CODING AND WHY IS IT IMPORTANT?

Coding is the process of writing instructions in a computer programming language to create software, applications, and other digital solutions. It involves writing code that a computer can understand and execute to perform a specific task or solve a problem. Coding is important because it provides a way for humans to communicate with computers and automate complex processes.

In today's world, technology plays a major role in our daily lives and coding is the backbone of many technological advancements. From smartphones and social media to e-commerce websites and financial systems, all of these rely on code to function. As technology continues to evolve, the demand for skilled coders only grows.

Coding also provides valuable skills and opportunities for personal and professional growth. It requires critical thinking, problem-solving, and creativity, all of which are valuable skills in a wide range of careers. Furthermore, the demand for coders and software developers is high, and there is a shortage of skilled professionals in many industries. This creates numerous job opportunities for those with coding skills and the ability to learn and adapt to new technologies.

In addition, coding is a valuable tool for personal projects and hobbies. Whether you want to create a website, build a mobile app, or automate a task, coding provides the tools to turn your ideas into reality. With coding, you have the power to create and innovate, and the possibilities are limited only by your imagination.

In conclusion, coding is an essential skill in today's world and provides numerous benefits both personally and professionally. Whether you want to pursue a career in technology or simply have a personal project you want to build, coding is a valuable tool to have.

CHAPTER TWO

Getting Started: Setting up your environment, downloading software and resources

Getting started with coding can be a bit intimidating, but with the right tools and resources, it can also be exciting and rewarding. In this chapter, we'll cover the basics of setting up your environment, downloading the necessary software and resources, and getting ready to start coding.

The first step in setting up your environment is to choose a computer. For coding, you'll need a computer that is capable of running the software and tools you'll be using. A laptop or desktop computer is recommended, but some coding can also be done on a tablet or smartphone.

Next, you'll need to choose a code editor. A code editor is a program that allows you to write, edit, and debug your code. There are many code editors available, both free and paid, and it's important to choose one that you're comfortable using. Some popular free code editors include Visual Studio Code, Atom, and Sublime Text.

Once you have your code editor set up, it's time to download any additional software and resources you'll need. This may include a web browser, a version control system like Git, and any software libraries or frameworks that you plan to use.

Additionally, it's important to set up a development environment. This can be done by creating a local development server, which allows you to run and test your code locally before deploying it to a live website or application. There are many tools available to help you set up a local development environment, including WAMP, XAMPP, and MAMP.

It's also a good idea to set up an online presence and start building your portfolio. This can be done by creating a personal website, starting a blog, or setting up a social media account specifically for your coding projects. Having a strong online presence will help you showcase your skills and projects to potential employers and other professionals in the field.

Finally, make sure to familiarize yourself with the resources available for learning and support. This includes online forums, coding communities, and online courses and tutorials. The coding community is friendly and supportive, and there are many resources available to help you learn and grow as a coder.

In conclusion, setting up your environment, downloading software and resources, and getting familiar with the resources available for learning and support are essential steps in getting started with coding. With the right tools and resources in place, you'll be well on your way to mastering the art of coding.

HTML
</>

CHAPTER THREE

The Basics: Understanding Variables, Data Types, and Basic Syntax

The basics of coding involve understanding variables, data types, and basic syntax. These concepts form the foundation of coding and are crucial for writing effective and efficient code. In this chapter, we'll cover these important topics in detail.

Variables are containers for storing data in your code. They allow you to store and manipulate data in your programs. Variables have a name and a value, and the value can change throughout the life of the program. For example, you can store a user's name in a variable, and then use that variable throughout your code to personalize the user's experience.

Data types are a way of categorizing the different types of data that can be stored in a variable. There are several data types in most programming languages, including numbers, strings, and boolean values. It's important to choose the right data type for your variables, as this can impact the performance and functionality of your code.

Basic syntax refers to the rules and structure of the programming language you're using. These rules determine how you write your code, and include things like the way you format your code, the way you use keywords and operators, and the way you use parentheses, brackets, and semicolons.

Variables can be declared using a specific syntax that varies depending on the programming language you're using. For example, in Python, you can declare a variable like this:

```
name = "John Doe"
```

Data types can be specified when you declare a variable, or they can be inferred automatically based on the value you assign to the variable. For example, the following code declares a variable with the string data type:

```
name = "John Doe"
```

In addition to data types, it's important to understand basic operators and expressions. Operators allow you to perform operations on variables and values, such as addition, subtraction, multiplication, and division. Expressions are combinations of variables, values, and operators that evaluate a single value.

For example, the following code declares two variables, **a** and **b**, and performs a calculation using the + operator:

```
a = 5
b = 3
c = a + b
```

In this example, the expression **a + b** evaluates to **8**, and the value is stored in the variable **c**.

It's also important to understand the use of control structures, such as if statements and loops. Control structures allow you to control the flow of your code and execute certain blocks of code only under specific conditions.

For example, the following code uses an if statement to check if a variable is equal to a certain value, and performs an action if the condition is met:

```
a = 5
if a == 5:
```

print("a is equal to 5")

In this example, the if statement checks if the value of the variable **a** is equal to **5**. If the condition is met, the code inside the if statement is executed and the message "**a is equal to 5**" is printed.

In conclusion, understanding variables, data types, and basic syntax is an important first step in coding. These concepts form the foundation of coding and provide the tools and knowledge you need to write effective and efficient code. By mastering these basics, you'll be well on your way to mastering the art of coding.

CHAPTER FOUR

Control Structures: Conditional Statements, Loops and Functions

Control structures are an important part of programming, allowing you to control the flow of your code and make decisions based on conditions. There are three main types of control structures: conditional statements, loops, and functions. In this chapter, we'll cover each of these in detail.

Conditional statements allow you to make decisions in your code based on conditions. For example, you might want to display a message only if a certain condition is met. The most common type of conditional statement is the if statement.

Here's an example of how you might use an if statement in Python:

```
a = 5
if a == 5:
print("a is equal to 5")
```

In this example, the if statement checks if the value of the variable **a** is equal to **5**. If the condition is met, the code inside the if statement is executed and the message "**a is equal to 5**" is printed.

In addition to if statements, you might also use other types of conditional statements, such as if-else statements and switch statements. An if-else statement allows you to specify an action to be taken if the condition is met, and an alternate action to be taken if the condition is not met. A switch statement allows you to specify multiple conditions and actions, making it useful for dealing with complex conditional logic.

Loops allow you to repeat a block of code a specified number of times. There are two main types of loops: for loops and while loops. A for loop is used to repeat a block of code a specific number of times, while a while loop is used to repeat a block of code as long as a certain condition is met.

Here's an example of how you might use a for loop in Python:

```
for i in range(5):
print(i)
```

In this example, the for loop will repeat the code inside the loop five times. On each iteration, the value of **i** will be updated to the next number in the range **(0, 1, 2, 3, 4)**.

Functions are a way to organize and reuse your code. Functions allow you to encapsulate a specific piece of code and reuse it multiple times throughout your program. Functions are defined using a specific syntax and can be called from anywhere in your code.

Here's an example of how you might define a function in Python:

```
def say_hello(name):
print("Hello, " + name)
say_hello("John")
```

In this example, the function **say_hello** takes one argument, **name**, and prints a message using the value of **name**. The function is defined using the **def** keyword, followed by the name of the function and the arguments it takes in parentheses. The code inside the function is indented and is executed when the function is called. In this case, the function is called with the argument "**John**".

In conclusion, control structures are an essential part of programming and allow you to control the flow of your code and make decisions based on conditions. Whether you're using if statements, loops, or functions, understanding how to use these structures will help you write more effective and efficient code.

CHAPTER FIVE

Object-Oriented Programming: Understanding Classes, Objects, and Inheritance

Object-oriented programming (OOP) is a programming paradigm that is based on the concept of objects. Objects are instances of classes, which are essentially templates for creating objects. Objects contain data, in the form of attributes, and behaviors, in the form of methods.

Classes are defined using the **class** keyword, followed by the name of the class. The body of the class is indented and contains the attributes and methods of the class. Attributes are variables that store data, while methods are functions that define the behaviors of the class.

Here's an example of a simple class in Python:

```
class Dog:
    def __init__(self, name, breed):
        self.name = name
        self.breed = breed

    def bark(self):
        print("Woof!")

dog = Dog("Fido", "Labrador")
dog.bark()
```

In this example, we define a class called **Dog** that has two attributes, **name** and **breed**, and one method, **bark**. The **__init__** method is a special method that is called when an object is created from the class. It is used to initialize the attributes of the object. In this case, we use the **__init__** method to set the values of **name** and **breed** for the **dog** object.

Once you have defined a class, you can create objects from it using the class name followed by parentheses. In this example, we create an object called **dog** using the **Dog** class. We can then access the attributes and call the methods of the object, just like we would with any other variable or function.

Inheritance is a feature of OOP that allows you to create a new class that is a modified version of an existing class. The new class, known as a subclass, inherits all of the attributes and methods of the parent class, known as the superclass. You can also add new attributes and methods to the subclass, or override methods of the superclass.

Here's an example of inheritance in Python:

```
class Animal:
    def __init__(self, name):
        self.name = name

    def make_sound(self):
        pass

class Dog(Animal):
    def make_sound(self):
        print("Woof!")

dog = Dog("Fido")
dog.make_sound()
```

In this example, we create a class called **Animal** that has an attribute **name** and a method **make_sound**. We then create a subclass called **Dog** that inherits from **Animal**. We override the **make_sound** method in the **Dog** class to print "Woof!" when called.

In conclusion, OOP is an important aspect of programming that allows you to model real-world objects in your code. Classes and objects provide a way to organize and reuse your code, while inheritance allows you to build on existing classes to create new, more specialized classes. Understanding OOP concepts will help you write more effective and maintainable code.

CHAPTER SIX

WEB DEVELOPMENT: HTML, CSS, AND JAVASCRIPT

Web development is the process of building and maintaining websites. The three main technologies used in web development are HTML, CSS, and JavaScript.

HTML, or HyperText Markup Language, is the standard markup language used to create web pages. HTML is used to structure the content of a web page, including text, images, and links. HTML tags are used to define the structure and content of a web page. For example, the <h1> tag is used to define a header, while the <p> tag is used to define a paragraph.

CSS, or Cascading Style Sheets, is used to style the content of a web page. CSS can be used to control the layout of a web page, including the position and size of elements, as well as the color, font, and background of elements. CSS can be written in separate files and linked to a web page, or it can be included directly in the HTML code of a web page.

JavaScript is a programming language that is used to make web pages dynamic and interactive. JavaScript can be used to add interactivity to a web page, such as responding to user actions, creating animations, and updating the content of a web page without requiring a page reload. JavaScript can be written directly in the HTML code of a web page or in separate JavaScript files.

Here's an example of a simple web page written in HTML, CSS, and JavaScript:

```
<!DOCTYPE html>
<html>
  <head>
    <style>
      .header {
        background-color: blue;
        color: white;
        padding: 20px;
        text-align: center;
      }
    </style>
  </head>
  <body>
    <div class="header">
      <h1>My Web Page</h1>
    </div>
    <p>Click the button to change the header color:</p>
    <button onclick="changeHeaderColor()">Change Color</button>
    <script>
      function changeHeaderColor() {
        const header = document.querySelector(".header");
        header.style.backgroundColor = "red";
      }
    </script>
  </body>
</html>
```

The example code given above can be broken down into three parts: **HTML, CSS**, and **JavaScript**.

HTML is used to define the structure and content of a web page. In the code, the HTML starts with a **<!DOCTYPE html>** declaration, which specifies that the document is written in HTML5. The **<html>** tag defines the start and end of the HTML document. Within the HTML document, there are two main sections, the **<head>** and **<body>** sections.

The **<head>** section contains information about the document, such as the title of the page and any external resources that are linked to the page, such as CSS and JavaScript files. In the code, the CSS is included directly in the **<head>** section, inside a **<style>** tag.

The **<body>** section contains the content that is displayed on the web page. In the code, the content is defined using HTML tags, such as the **<div>** tag, which defines a block-level element, and the **<p>** tag, which defines a paragraph. The **<button>** tag is used to create a button that the user can interact with. The onclick attribute is used to specify a JavaScript function that will be executed when the button is clicked.

CSS is used to style the content of a web page. In the code, the CSS is included in the **<head>** section, inside a **<style>** tag. The CSS rules are defined using selectors, such as the **.header** class selector, and properties, such as the **background-color** and **color** properties. The CSS rules define the styles that will be applied to the HTML elements on the web page.

JavaScript is used to make the web page dynamic and interactive. In the code, JavaScript is included at the end of the **<body>** section, inside a **<script>** tag. The JavaScript function, **changeHeaderColor**, is defined using the **function** keyword. The function changes the background color of the **.header** class when it is executed.

To connect HTML, CSS, and JavaScript, we need to reference the HTML elements in the CSS and JavaScript code. In the CSS, we use the **.header** class selector to target the **<div>** element with the class of **header**. In JavaScript, we use the **document.querySelector** method to select the **<div>** element with the class of **header** and change its **backgroundColor** property. This is how the styles defined in the CSS are applied to the HTML elements, and how the JavaScript can interact with and manipulate the content of the web page.

In conclusion, HTML, CSS, and JavaScript are the building blocks of the web, and they work together to create the websites that we use every day. By learning these technologies, you can build your own websites, add interactivity to your web pages, and bring your ideas to life on the web.

CHAPTER SEVEN

DATABASES: SQL AND WORKING WITH DATABASES

Databases are essential components of many software applications. They provide a way to store and manage large amounts of data in a structured way. **SQL (Structured Query Language)** is the most widely used language for working with databases. It is a standard language used to manage and manipulate relational databases.

In a relational database, data is organized into tables, with each table containing rows and columns. SQL is used to create and modify these tables, as well as to insert, update, and retrieve data from them. For example, the **CREATE TABLE** statement is used to create a new table, while the **INSERT INTO** statement is used to insert data into a table. The **SELECT** statement is used to retrieve data from a table, and the **UPDATE** statement is used to update existing data.

SQL also provides many advanced features for working with databases. For example, it includes support for transactions, which allow multiple operations to be executed as a single, atomic unit of work. Transactions ensure that the database remains in a consistent state even if an error occurs during the execution of the operations. SQL also provides support for data constraints, which enforce rules on the data stored in the database, such as unique constraints that ensure that a specific column only contains unique values.

When working with databases, it's important to understand the basics of SQL syntax and the structure of relational databases. The SQL syntax consists of keywords and clauses that are used to perform different operations on the database. For example, the **FROM** clause is used to specify the table that data should be retrieved from, while the **WHERE** clause is used to specify conditions that the data must meet.

There are many different database management systems (DBMS) that support SQL, such as MySQL, PostgreSQL, and Microsoft SQL Server. These DBMS provide a variety of tools and interfaces for working with databases, including command-line interfaces, graphical user interfaces, and programming APIs.

here's a simple SQL code example for creating a database table and inserting data into it:

```
CREATE TABLE users (
  id INT PRIMARY KEY AUTO_INCREMENT,
  name VARCHAR(50) NOT NULL,
  email VARCHAR(255) NOT NULL,
  created_at DATETIME DEFAULT CURRENT_TIMESTAMP
);

INSERT INTO users (name, email)
VALUES ('John Doe', 'john.doe@example.com'),
       ('Jane Doe', 'jane.doe@example.com');
```

Let me explain the code:

1. **CREATE TABLE** users - This line creates a new table called "users".
2. **idINT PRIMARY KEY AUTO_INCREMENT** - This line defines a column called "id" which is an integer data type. The **PRIMARY KEY** and **AUTO_INCREMENT** keywords are used to create a unique identifier for each row in the table. The **AUTO_INCREMENT** keyword ensures that the value of the "id" column is automatically incremented for each new row.

3. **name VARCHAR(50) NOT NULL** - This line defines a column called "name" which is a string data type with a maximum length of 50 characters. The **NOT NULL** keyword ensures that a value must be provided for this column.
4. **email VARCHAR(255) NOT NULL** - This line defines a column called "email" which is a string data type with a maximum length of 255 characters. The **NOT NULL** keyword ensures that a value must be provided for this column.
5. **created_at DATETIME DEFAULT CURRENT_TIMESTAMP** - This line defines a column called "created_at" which is a date and time data type. The **DEFAULT CURRENT_TIMESTAMP** keyword ensures that the current date and time will be automatically inserted into this column for each new row.
6. **INSERT INTO users (name, email)** - This line inserts new rows into the "users" table. The columns being inserted into are specified in the parentheses, in this case "name" and "email".
7. **VALUES ('John Doe', 'john.doe@example.com'), ('Jane Doe', 'jane.doe@example.com')** - This line provides the values for the columns being inserted. Two rows are being inserted, one for "John Doe" and one for "Jane Doe".

This code demonstrates the basic syntax for creating a database table and inserting data into it using SQL. Of course, there is much more to learn about SQL and working with databases, but this example should give you a good starting point.

In conclusion, databases and SQL are critical components of many software applications, and understanding the basics of databases and SQL is essential for any software developer. Whether you're building a web application, a mobile app, or any other type of software, having a solid understanding of databases and SQL will help you build more robust and scalable applications.

CHAPTER EIGHT

Debugging: Common Issues and How to Troubleshoot and Fix Them

Debugging is an important part of the software development process, as it involves finding and fixing errors in your code. Debugging can be a challenging task, but with the right tools and techniques, it can be made easier.

Here are some common issues that developers encounter while coding and how to troubleshoot and fix them:

1. **Syntax errors** - These are errors in the structure of the code, such as missing punctuation, misspelled keywords, or incorrect use of quotes. To troubleshoot syntax errors, check the code against the language's syntax rules and look for any discrepancies.
2. **Logic errors** - These are errors in the logic of the code, such as incorrect use of conditions, loops, or variables. To troubleshoot logic errors, use a combination of print statements, comments, and breakpoints to trace the flow of the code and understand what's going wrong.
3. **Run-time errors** - These are errors that occur when the code is running, such as division by zero, null pointer exceptions, or index out of bounds errors. To troubleshoot run-time errors, use the error messages provided

by the debugger to identify the source of the error, and use print statements or breakpoints to understand the flow of the code.

4. **Semantic errors** - These are errors in the meaning of the code, such as incorrect use of functions, variables, or objects. To troubleshoot semantic errors, use print statements or breakpoints to understand the values of variables and objects at different points in the code.

Here are some examples of how to troubleshoot and fix these common issues:

1. Syntax error example:

for i in range(10)
print(i)

In this example, the syntax error is caused by a missing colon at the end of the for loop. To fix this error, add a colon to the end of the for loop:

for i in range(10):
print(i)

2. Logic error example:

```
def divide(a, b):
  return a / b

result = divide(10, 2)
print(result)
```

In this example, the logic error is caused by not handling the case where **b** is equal to zero. To fix this error, add a check to the divide function to handle this case:

```
def divide(a, b):
  if b == 0:
    return "Cannot divide by zero"
  return a / b

result = divide(10, 2)
print(result)
```

3. Run-time error example:

```
numbers = [1, 2, 3, 4, 5]
print(numbers[10])
```

In this example, the run-time error is caused by trying to access an index that is out of bounds of the **numbers** list. To fix this error, add a check to make sure that the index being accessed is within the bounds of the list:

```
numbers = [1, 2, 3, 4, 5]
if 10 < len(numbers):
  print(numbers[10])
else:
  print("Index out of bounds")
```

Debugging can be a time-consuming process, but with practice and the right techniques, you can make it easier. By understanding the types of errors that can occur and using debugging tools, such as print statements, the debugger, and logging, you can quickly identify and fix issues in your code. It is also important to develop a systematic approach to debugging, such as reproducing the error, identifying the source of the problem, and testing potential solutions. Additionally, having a clear understanding of the logic and structure of your code can also greatly aid in the debugging process.

It's also worth mentioning that debugging is an iterative process and often requires trial and error. Don't be discouraged if you can't find the solution right away. Instead, take a step back, review your code and approach, and try a different technique. And remember, seeking help from others, whether it's from a mentor, colleague, or online community, can also be a valuable resource in debugging.

Overall, debugging is a crucial part of the coding process and helps you to write clean, efficient, and error-free code. With practice and the right tools and techniques, you can become a more efficient and confident coder.

CHAPTER NINE

BEST PRACTICES: CLEAN CODE, DOCUMENTATION, AND WORKING IN A TEAM

Coding is a complex process that requires a combination of technical skills, attention to detail, and the ability to think logically. However, these skills alone are not enough to ensure that your code is effective and easy to maintain. That's why it's important to adopt best practices when coding to ensure that your code is clean and well-documented and that you are working effectively in a team environment.

Clean Code

Clean code is code that is easy to read, understand, and maintain. The benefits of clean code are many, including easier debugging, better collaboration, and improved efficiency. To write clean code, you should aim to follow a consistent style, choose meaningful variable names, use comments to explain what your code does and structure your code in a logical way. Additionally, you should avoid writing overly complex code and aim to write code that is easy to test and maintain.

Documentation

Documentation is an essential part of any software project. It provides an overview of the system, explains how it works, and provides information about how to use it. Good documentation can also help you keep track of the changes you make to your code and can help others understand your code. To write good documentation, you should aim to explain what your code does, use examples to illustrate your points, and provide a clear and concise overview of the system. Additionally, you should aim to keep your documentation up to date and make it easy to find.

Working in a Team

Collaboration is an important part of software development, and working effectively in a team can help you produce better results. To work effectively in a team, you should aim to communicate clearly and effectively, share your work, and provide feedback on the work of others. Additionally, you should aim to stay organized and use tools like version control systems, project management software, and issue trackers to help you collaborate with others.

In conclusion, clean code, documentation, and working in a team are all essential best practices for software development. By following these best practices, you can ensure that your code is of high quality, easy to maintain and that you are working effectively in a team environment. So, make sure to adopt these best practices and continuously work on improving your coding skills and knowledge.

CHAPTER TEN

DSA: Data Structures and Algorithms

Data Structures and Algorithms (DSA) are the backbone of computer science and a critical component of coding. Understanding DSA is essential for anyone who wants to develop efficient and effective solutions to complex problems. This chapter will cover the fundamental concepts of DSA and how to apply them in real-world situations.

The algorithms that are used in DSA are:

1. **Sorting algorithms:** This includes algorithms such as bubble sort, insertion sort, quick sort, merge sort, etc. These algorithms are used to sort arrays of data in ascending or descending order.
2. **Searching algorithms:** This includes algorithms such as linear search, binary search, and hash tables. These algorithms are used to search for elements in a data structure.
3. Graph algorithms: This includes algorithms such as breadth-first search, depth-first search, minimum spanning tree, and shortest path. These algorithms are used to work with graph data structures.
4. **Dynamic programming algorithms:** This includes algorithms such as the knapsack problem, the traveling salesman problem, and the longest common subsequence problem. These algorithms are used to solve problems with overlapping subproblems.
5. **Divide and conquer algorithms:** This includes algorithms such as the merge sort, quick sort, and the closest pair of points problem. These

algorithms are used to solve problems by breaking them down into smaller subproblems.

6. **Greedy algorithms:** This includes algorithms such as the activity selection problem, the fractional knapsack problem, and the huffman coding. These algorithms are used to solve problems by making the locally optimal choice at each step.

Data Structures are also a way of organizing and storing data in a computer so that it can be accessed and modified efficiently. They provide a framework for organizing data, and they form the building blocks of many algorithms. Some of the most common data structures include:

1. **Arrays:** A collection of elements stored in contiguous memory locations. They are used to store homogeneous elements and are easy to access randomly.
2. **Linked Lists:** A linear data structure where elements are not stored in contiguous memory locations but are connected by pointers. They are useful for dynamic memory allocation.
3. **Stacks:** A Last-In-First-Out (LIFO) data structure where the most recently added item is the first one to be removed. They are used to implement undo/redo operations.
4. **Queues:** A First-In-First-Out (FIFO) data structure where the first item to be added is the first one to be removed. They are used to implement processes waiting in line for execution.
5. **Trees:** A hierarchical data structure with a root node, branches, and leaves. They are used to represent hierarchical relationships and to implement efficient search algorithms.
6. **Graphs:** A collection of nodes and edges that can represent complex relationships. They are used to model real-world systems and to solve problems such as finding the shortest path.

Algorithms are step-by-step procedures for solving problems. Sorting algorithms are used to arrange elements in a particular order while searching algorithms are used to find elements in a data structure. Some common algorithms include:

- Sorting algorithms: QuickSort, MergeSort, InsertionSort, BubbleSort
- Searching algorithms: Linear Search, Binary Search, Depth-First Search, Breadth-First Search

By studying these data structures and algorithms, you can gain a deeper understanding of how to store, access, and manipulate data efficiently, and how to solve problems in a more efficient and effective way.

CHAPTER ELEVEN

Advanced Topics: Artificial Intelligence, Machine Learning, and Game Development

Artificial intelligence, machine learning, and game development are some of the most exciting and rapidly evolving areas of computer science and software development. In this section, we will take an in-depth look at these three areas and how they can be applied to create innovative and impactful solutions.

Artificial Intelligence:

Artificial Intelligence (AI) is a branch of computer science that focuses on creating machines and algorithms that can perform tasks that would normally require human intelligence, such as visual perception, speech recognition, decision-making, and language translation. AI technologies are built on the foundations of machine learning, where computers learn from data, and computer vision, where machines can interpret and understand images and videos.

In recent years, AI has become increasingly prevalent in various industries, including finance, healthcare, retail, and transportation. For example, AI-powered chatbots can provide 24/7 customer support, AI algorithms can be used to analyze medical images to detect diseases, and AI-powered personal assistants can help users manage their schedules and tasks.

To get started with AI, you'll need a solid foundation in mathematics, statistics, and programming. You can then choose to specialize in areas such as computer vision, natural language processing, or deep learning.

Machine Learning:

Machine Learning (ML) is a subset of AI that involves training computer algorithms to learn patterns in data and make predictions based on that data. ML algorithms can be supervised, unsupervised, or semi-supervised, depending on the type of data and the desired outcome.

For example, supervised machine learning algorithms are used for classification and regression problems, where the algorithm is trained on labeled data to make predictions about future data. Unsupervised machine learning algorithms, on the other hand, are used for clustering and dimensionality reduction, where the algorithm tries to find structure in unlabeled data.

To get started with machine learning, you'll need a solid foundation in mathematics, statistics, and programming. You can then choose to specialize in areas such as deep learning, computer vision, or natural language processing.

Game Development:

Game development involves the creation of video games, from the initial concept to the final product. Game developers use a variety of tools and technologies, including game engines, programming languages, and graphic design software, to bring their ideas to life.

Game development can be divided into several stages, including game design, programming, testing, and deployment. Game designers are responsible for creating the overall vision for the game, including the story, characters, and gameplay mechanics. Programmers then use programming languages such as C++ or Python to create the game logic and bring the design to life.

To get started with game development, you'll need a solid foundation in programming and computer graphics. You can then choose to specialize in areas such as game design, programming, or art and animation. There are many resources available to help you get started, including online tutorials, courses, and game development communities.

Whether you are interested in AI, machine learning, game development, or all three, it is important to understand the fundamentals and best practices in these areas. In conclusion, these three advanced topics are highly important and have a huge impact on the world of technology. Artificial intelligence, machine learning, and game development are constantly evolving and offer a wide range of opportunities for those who are interested in pursuing a career in these fields. Whether you are a seasoned software developer or just starting out, understanding these topics will give you a solid foundation for a successful career in the tech industry.

CHAPTER TWELVE

Project Development: A Step by Step Guide to Developing a Complete Project from Start to Finish

Project development is a crucial aspect of the software development process. It involves taking a concept or idea and transforming it into a functioning and useful product. This process requires careful planning, execution, and attention to detail to ensure a successful outcome. Whether you're a beginner or an experienced software developer, this guide will provide you with a step-by-step guide to developing a complete project from start to finish.

Step 1: **Ideation and Conceptualization**

The first step in developing a project is to come up with an idea. This could be an idea for a new software application, a website, or a mobile app. Once you have an idea, the next step is to research and validate your concept. This involves understanding the target audience, conducting market research, and determining the feasibility of your project.

Step 2: **Planning and Requirements Gathering**

Once you have validated your idea, the next step is to plan and gather requirements. This involves creating a detailed project plan that outlines the project timeline, resources needed, and project milestones. You should also gather detailed requirements for the project, including functional requirements, performance requirements, and any other constraints.

Step 3: **Design and Architecture**

After planning and gathering requirements, the next step is to design the architecture of the project. This involves creating a high-level design of the project, including the user interface, data model, and any other relevant components. The design should be clear, simple, and easy to understand.

Step 4: **Development and Implementation**

With the design and architecture in place, the next step is to start development and implementation. This involves writing the code and developing the various components of the project. It's important to follow best practices for coding and to use version control software to keep track of changes and maintain the stability of the project.

Step 5: **Testing and Quality Assurance**

Once the development is complete, the next step is to perform testing and quality assurance. This involves running various tests to ensure that the project meets the requirements and works as intended. This could include unit testing, integration testing, and functional testing.

Step 6: **Deployment and Maintenance**

The final step in the project development process is deployment and maintenance. This involves deploying the project to a production environment, ensuring that it's up and running, and maintaining it over time. This could involve fixing bugs, adding new features, and ensuring that the project continues to perform well.

In conclusion, project development is a complex process that requires careful planning, execution, and attention to detail. By following the steps outlined in this guide, you can ensure a successful outcome for your project and deliver high-quality software that meets the needs of your users.

CHAPTER THIRTEEN

Open Source: Contributing to Open Source Projects

Open-source projects are an essential part of the software development community, providing free access to powerful tools and platforms for developers around the world. Contributing to open-source projects is a great way to give back to the community, enhance your coding skills, and build a strong network of professional connections.

Getting started with open-source contributions can be a bit overwhelming, but it is a rewarding experience that can benefit you in many ways. This chapter will cover some of the basics of open-source contribution and help you get started with your first contribution.

Step 1: **Find a project that interests you**

The first step to contributing to an open-source project is to find one that interests you. There are many different open-source projects available, ranging from simple scripts to complex platforms. You can find open-source projects on websites such as GitHub, GitLab, and Bitbucket.

Step 2: **Read the documentation**

Before you start contributing, it is important to familiarize yourself with the project and its goals. You should read the project's documentation and understand the scope of the project and the technologies it uses. You should also familiarize yourself with the project's contribution guidelines and coding standards.

Step 3: **Make a contribution**

Once you have familiarized yourself with the project, you can start making contributions. This could include fixing bugs, adding new features, or improving documentation. It is important to make small, incremental changes at first and get feedback from the project maintainers.

Step 4: **Join the community**

Contributing to an open-source project is not just about making code contributions, it's also about being part of a community. You should join the project's mailing list, participate in discussions, and attend community events. This will help you build relationships with other contributors and learn more about the project.

In conclusion, contributing to open-source projects is a great way to build your coding skills, give back to the community, and make professional connections. It can be a bit intimidating at first, but with a little effort and persistence, anyone can become a successful open-source contributor.

CHAPTER FOURTEEN

GIT & GITHUB: FUNDAMENTALS OF GIT & GITHUB

Git and GitHub are essential tools for modern software development. Git is a distributed version control system that helps developers manage and track changes to source code. GitHub, on the other hand, is a web-based platform that provides hosting for Git repositories and a range of tools for collaboration and code review.

In this chapter, we will cover the basics of Git and GitHub and how they are used in software development.

Git Fundamentals

Git is a decentralized version control system that allows developers to manage and track changes to their code. It works by keeping a record of changes made to the codebase over time, allowing developers to easily switch between different versions of their code. Git also supports collaboration by allowing multiple developers to work on the same codebase simultaneously.

Getting Started with GitHub

GitHub is a web-based platform that provides hosting for Git repositories and a range of tools for collaboration and code review. To get started with GitHub, you need to create a free account and set up a repository for your project. A repository is a place where you can store your code and collaborate with other developers.

Working with Git and GitHub Once you have set up a repository on GitHub, you can start working with Git to manage your code. This typically involves creating a local copy of your repository on your computer, making changes to your code and then pushing those changes back to the repository on GitHub.

Git and GitHub also provide a range of tools for collaboration and code review, including pull requests, issues, and wikis. Pull requests allow you to share your changes with other developers and get feedback, while issues are a place to discuss problems and track progress. Wikis provide a place to document your project and share information with others.

In conclusion, Git and GitHub are powerful tools that play a central role in modern software development. By learning to use these tools, you can improve your productivity, collaborate more effectively with other developers, and deliver higher-quality software.

CHAPTER FIFTEEN

Conclusion: Recap of the Key Concepts and Advice for Continuing Your Coding Journey

In the concluding chapter of "Coding: A Beginner's Guide to Mastering the Art," it's important to summarize the key concepts that have been covered throughout the book. This chapter should also offer advice for readers who are looking to continue their coding journey and take their skills to the next level.

Recapping the key concepts means discussing the most important topics that were covered in each chapter. This could include things like setting up your development environment, understanding variables and data types, working with control structures like conditional statements and loops, object-oriented programming, web development, databases, debugging, and best practices. By summarizing these key concepts, readers will be able to quickly reference what they've learned and continue building on their knowledge.

Advice for continuing the coding journey should also be provided in this chapter. This could include recommendations for resources such as books, online courses, or communities that can help readers continue their education. It's also important to discuss the importance of practice, experimentation, and collaboration in the development of coding skills.

Additionally, it's important to encourage readers to take on projects and work on real-world problems, as this will help them apply the concepts they've learned and develop their skills. Finally, it's important to emphasize that coding is a lifelong journey and there is always more to learn and explore in this field.

In conclusion, the final chapter of "Coding: A Beginner's Guide to Mastering the Art" should summarize the key concepts covered throughout the book, offer advice for continuing the coding journey, and encourage readers to continue learning and developing their skills

Thank You

In this book, we have covered the basics of coding and explored the different paths that you can take on your journey as a programmer. Whether you are just starting out or looking to expand your knowledge, the information in this book provides a solid foundation for building your skills.

We have discussed the different programming languages and the roles they play in the development of software, as well as the basics of data structures and algorithms and how they are used to solve problems. We have also covered Git and GitHub, which are essential tools for modern software development.

Now that you have a roadmap for learning to code, the next step is to put your knowledge into practice. Start by working on small projects and experimenting with different languages and tools. As you gain experience, you can move on to more complex projects and continue to develop your skills.

Remember, coding is a continuous learning process, and there is always room for improvement. Stay curious, stay motivated, and never stop learning. With persistence and dedication, you can achieve your goals and become a successful programmer.

Good luck on your journey, and happy coding!

www.ingramcontent.com/pod-product-compliance
Ingram Content Group UK Ltd.
Pitfield, Milton Keynes, MK11 3LW, UK
UKHW022009190726
13853UKWH00004B/1840